ARISTOTLE IN TESTING

The most enjoyable way to learn hard hitting testing lessons through analogies that even people with 2 decades in IT fail to learn

PRADEEP SOUNDARARAJAN

notionpress.com

INDIA • SINGAPORE • MALAYSIA

ISBN 979-8-90362-648-9

Contents

The Vision for This Book

Aristotle in Testing is going to be one of the easiest and most enjoyable books to read in Testing.

Having published Buddha in Testing and sold a few thousand copies of it, combined with the Amazon reviews, LinkedIn posts, emails, and many DMs from people who bought the book, I found that people actually finished reading (not just buying) the book. It is a milestone because buying the book doesn't always mean reading it and doesn't always mean completing it. Equally, I loved that the readers of Buddha in Testing appreciated the simplicity as a key factor for having completed reading it and understanding it well enough to be touched by it. Many claimed they now have a way to find their inner peace in their testing life, having read the book. That's truly what I wanted to deliver through the book. It ended up becoming a bigger success than I expected, given that it was my first published book and I had the least expectations with it.

Years later, I took a bold step to publish another book, for a very serious and passionate audience, titled "Growth-Driven Testing," which sold a few thousand copies, too. However, I found that many people struggled to complete reading the book because it was deep, hard to digest, and dealt with complex subjects around testing in a way that the reader has to think, disagree, debate, and then digest. "Buddha in Testing," on the other hand, was a cool breeze of air on a beautiful summer day. All they needed to do was to slightly put their head out to experience it.

These two books, their writing styles, their readership, and reviews provided a valuable insight to me as to how modern-day people are when it comes to reading a book. The passionate ones still do read complex stuff and enjoy it, but the large masses of testers are people living in the land of distractions and notifications. To them, reading a book and completing it is hard, and equally, they know that they do survive professionally without reading books. They are going about their jobs, promotions, and hikes. So reading a book is not compelling enough.

Passion for testing is dwindling. Passion for everything that surrounds testing is increasing. Also, because the number of people reading about testing is dwindling. Most people today want reels, not a good collection of books. Most people on this Earth today have a saved collection of reels rather than books they bought in the last twenty-four months.

Also, the Gen Zs are wired differently. They are overwhelmed with stuff happening, and they don't have time for long reads. In other words, in their no cap life, long reads aren't their vibe, and to make it fire for them, millennials like me gotta make books lit. To slay a testing book for them, I gotta come across as a face card of writing in testing. Icl ts.

I asked myself, how can I still get a lot of people (not just the usual suspects) to read a book on testing, enjoy it, and have something that touches them for a long time?

What if every paragraph were a short reel?

What if a bunch of reel-type paragraphs, stitched together as a chapter, can deliver the profoundness of a chapter from a good book?

What if reading this whole book is as fast and as easy as watching reels on TikTok, Instagram, or YouTube Shorts over a weekend?

What if this book helps many people cross the bridge to start reading other books, or for people to write books that are easier to read?

Can I?

Only you can tell.

I can only try and speculate.

This book cover is designed by Padmashree and Shree. Padmashree designed the cover for Buddha in Testing, and the world has loved it. Shree and Padmashree, a powerful design-thinking couple, have woven this wonderful cover design and also laid out the illustrations and styling of this book to enhance readers' experience. The good people of

Notion Press who took care of the publishing and distribution deserve a mention as all my books, including this one, are published through them. Quality always has many parents. I live in gratitude toward them.

Special Dedication

In 2009, I was working toward my first book attempt titled "Dumbugs" - a software testing fiction that had a plot on how aliens realize that in any physical form, humans will be able to defeat them, and to conquer Earth, those aliens have to take an invisible form. Some aliens figure out that many bugs in software aren't getting fixed, and that is the invisible form they want to take to cause disaster through software. Planes crash, stock market tanks, trillions of dollars of market cap of several top companies vanish, and the world is on the brink of a civil war. Two passionate software testers tasked to test radar software in a secret military area notice an anomaly that has a signature of a software bug, but also behaves differently, and it gets dismissed (I mean, who doesn't dismiss what testers report) and laughed at.

These two testers investigate the anomaly further, to then discover that those bugs are aliens. They fight the system and government to get those bugs fixed in all software that runs the world. The way they investigate and isolate bugs from alien bugs is a fantastic educational piece for software testers on how to test, investigate, isolate, and persist in getting a bug fixed. Their heroic story makes the world introduce a new form of software security guidelines, preventing another alien attack on this Earth through bugs.

Isn't that a fascinating, fun way to learn testing by reading fiction? I strongly believe we need to bring the fun back to testing. Most people wearing suits and guiding testing have removed the pure joy that once existed in testing software.

I needed a noble soul to help me review the chapters as I wrote them, and Maik Nogens from Hamburg, Germany, supported me quite a lot. He gave a lot of his time to me. He was patient and compassionate toward my writing and read through several iterations of certain chapters. He corrected my grammar and suggested good edits. However, as I wrote more and more chapters, I realized I am not suited to write fiction, and I dropped the idea of publishing this book. I informed the decision, thanked Maik, and forgot his existence. I think Maik deserved great recognition in the books I published later in life, but I failed to. I miserably failed. I want to fix it. Maik, this book is dedicated to you for the great support you offered to that young kid who wanted to publish his first book. People like you are the support system that makes people like me possible. I live in gratitude toward you. I am who I am also because of you.

In the same year, Melissa Pontes, then a tester from Brazil and now a Product Manager and Test Consultant, was in touch with me, exchanging thoughts and ideas in Testing regularly. When she learned that I was out of a job and was working on the book, she surprised me by asking me if she could transfer some money to me to support me in writing the book (while I was out of a job). She offered a month's worth of my salary, saying she could only afford that. I was deeply touched and did not take the money. Yet, it had a deep impact on me. As time passed by and I got busy with my business, I forgot about her and her act of kindness and lived a blind life.

When my vision was restored, I could see the profound impact people like Maik Nogens and Melissa Pontes had made on my life. They have made me, and hence this book, possible.

Melissa, what you offered wasn't money and support. It was a transformation to make me more human than I was back then. It is people like you and your genuine act of kindness that make people like me possible. I am who I am also because of you.

Also, dear readers, expressing gratitude is the highest form of living I have discovered. We get busy, and time makes us forget people who have truly transformed us at our soul level. We rest in peace when alive, only when we express gratitude to people who make us possible.

Who are the Maik Nogens and Melissa Pontes of your life? Don't become the Pradeep who forgot them; become the Pradeep who expressed gratitude.

Why Aristotle and Analogies?

Analogies are one of the easiest ways to understand something when we already know something else. In my little search and study, I found that Aristotle is considered to be the father of analogies. He promoted, evangelized, spoke, and gave a formal approach to using analogies to explain complex things for more people to connect and understand.

I am sure many people before that did too, but Aristotle did it consciously and with an intent, with consistency, to get identified as a father of analogies by people who came years after him and the wise souls that lived alongside him. So let us consider him as the modern worldwide popular name father of analogies, and there could be ancient fathers and mothers of analogies whom we don't know.

In my imagination, if Aristotle were alive and he were a tester and had written a book, this is the kind of book he would have written to help people who seem to be pretending they know it but need something like this to acknowledge and transform. He would have also written such a book for people who want to learn without flexing their minds, to help them see the beauty and nuances of testing. That's my imagination, and that's why Aristotle in Testing title became apt.

Equally, in this life, I have explained complex things through analogies, and people seemed to have an expression that they got it when they heard it or read it. Their search sometimes ended because of the analogy they heard from me, and this felt very satisfying to me as a person who wants to help people learn something deep through their own depth of understanding of certain subjects.

Analogies are hard to land, but if they do, they land so well, people will never forget it, and if it doesn't land well, I would have to go looking for a black box. That's the risk I took to write this book. That said, I had immense fun writing this book. I am also going to experience the joy of reading it as a book once published.

Writing and publishing are similar to pregnancy and childbirth. There's pain, joy, sleepless nights, anxiety, and responsibility. As I am writing this sentence, I am in my last trimester of my third baby (this book).

Context

No testing book has had chapters like this one has. I mean, imagine Formula 1 and Fishing being chapters in a testing book. It is crazy, out of the box, and intriguing, right? Of course, this is the first of its kind because this is Aristotle's first book in testing. The chapters are born out of either my first-hand experience or witnessing something for a long time in close quarters.

I have been watching Formula 1 since 2006. I have been playing Table Tennis since I was a twelve-year-old kid. I spent a few years in sport fishing Mahseer and Tilapias, catching and releasing them safely without killing them. Similarly, when you read some content like divorce and air crashes, don't assume I went through it :) I love my wife, and she loves me. Oh, and she is in the business of baking too, so the chapter of baking fits in well. I had a sports injury and needed help from a physiotherapist. The chapter on Sport Injury and Rehab was born with the help of Arpitha Rajagopal, who is a Master Physiotherapist. I have done hours of meditation at a time and prolonged, consistent yoga practice, hence the chapter on it. Also, Aristotle told me to write about certain topics, and he said you will enjoy reading it. I just obliged to his request.

I wish reading this book triggers your own Aristotle in Testing.

Long live Aristotle!

May you awaken the good souls living within you.

AI Disclaimer

The era we live in demands this disclaimer, unfortunately.

I did not use ChatGPT to write this.

Honestly, I tried taking help in a two-hour attempt, but it kept suggesting things that didn't go well with the experience and value I wanted you to have when reading this book.

I do use ChatGPT otherwise in my life.

Not to write.

More like a modern-day Google Search.

"Identify this bird in the pic I uploaded" types.

Like you, I am trying to find the context AI truly fits in and the context I should not fit it in, even if it appears to work.

At work, we have built a platform called Bugasura Testpert that uses AI to help in deep thinking, contextual testing suitable for test experts to operate and deliver growth-driven testing. The results, outside of the bias that I am involved in it, are impressive enough. Especially when I see the clients' quality standards growing with the platform and hence their business metrics. I do believe in AI, but I don't believe in how the world is trying to apply it to various things as the best way forward. I am Jojo, standing on a speck in Horton Hears a Who, and my opinion does not matter to this world unless I find Horton.

AI is like a cat that appeared for the first time in the world. We humans, are trying to identify if it should be left in the forest and admired for its beauty because it is a tiger, or brought home and treated like a pet cat because a tiger is a cat, anyway, with the risk of being eaten by the tiger someday.

Also, a very important disclaimer.

I use em dashes, these ones "-" a lot.

I used them even before ChatGPT came.

So, don't get carried away with my em dashes if you see them in this book or any writing of mine in the future.

Sit back, relax, grab a sip and enjoy this book.

It is written to enjoy.

It is written with a lot of joy.

Everything else is a side effect and your own derivation.

Driving

Driving

An expert car driver, who is sitting next to a novice driver in a car, goes through a tremendous amount of stress, similar to an expert tester in a team driven by a leader who is a novice in testing but an expert in programming.

Having good tools to enable testing and a good number of expert testers in an organization that requires too many approvals for simple things produces the same result as paying an expert driver to drive a Ferrari in Bangalore traffic conditions.

We should only automate testing completely, similar to how Waymo or Tesla did with car driving, by allocating a large budget to fight lawsuits in case of accidents.

The gear shift is automated, and the whole car is misleadingly branded as "automatic," similar to how a small portion of tests are automated, and the company claims that they do fully automated testing.

Driving is super fun, especially on long drives under good road conditions, traveling through scenic locations while the weather is pleasant, and people in the car are fun-loving. Similar to how testing is fun under leadership that understands the value of testing, focus is on customer value and not on pleasing people internally, and sufficient budget is allocated while people have a shared vision. How often do such drives happen?

A car that is built for safety is not built for speed, and a car that is built for speed is not built for luxury, similar to how a testing team that is built to reduce support cost may not be built for automation. Leaders who want the test team to be built for all purposes get nothing out of them and hence cut costs to not make their own mistakes visible to the board and shareholders.

Most cars these days have different modes of driving, such as economy, sports, and off-road, linking to fuel consumption and traction depending on the mode selected. Unlike in testing, the leaders want the same fuel spend while going off-road and driving in sports mode as they get in economy mode.

Insurance is mandatory for everyone who owns a car, and testing is the insurance for those who are building and owning a software product. The larger the premium, the more the coverage. Cars can be driven without insurance, of course.

When cars become an extension of an owner's ego, a small scratch can cause a huge blow to the ego, similar to how some leaders, whose engineering practices become an extension of their ego, and a bug in production puts a huge hole in their emotional stability.

In the name of cutting budgets in testing, sometimes management cuts important things based on data that is true and misleading. For example, the management asks a driver, "How often have you used a windshield wiper in the last six months as opposed to a brake pad?" and let's say the reply is, "Only eighteen days in the last three hundred and sixty-five days." The management makes a decision to get rid of the windshield wiper because the cost of replacing it is just a hundred dollars anyway, in case they need it.

A car that hasn't gone through regular maintenance is the one we most likely see on a highway with the bonnet up, similar to how software products that haven't been sufficiently maintained are the ones that end up needing more patches and bug fix releases frequently.

A car accident is like a bug in production. The customer is the most affected person from an injury perspective. The car manufacturer is the least affected, irrespective of how much stress they claim to exhibit. Good manufacturers care for customers and hence build the car to limit damage to their customers in case of an accident.

The majority of the decision weightage for most people choosing a car is also based on after-sales service, similar to how software product customers and users abandon good-looking software because the support sucks.

It is a tradition in the car industry to make claims of mileage of the car per full fuel or full charge based on ideal road conditions that never exist, similar to how many companies test their software in a test environment that is far off from the environment of their customers.

In the software world, there are dedicated management people to look at the windshield, and dedicated people to look at the rear-view mirror, both guiding the driver through their prompts by assuming the driver is blind. Such projects move slowly because the driver has to cater to everyone, including themselves.

Driving a car requires a high level of situational awareness. Talking or texting on the phone reduces situational awareness and creates distraction, leading to accidents. In the software world, slacking while working reduces situational awareness, and it has become a new norm to talk on the phone while driving.

Toyota cars are built for long-term quality, but have a boring outlook similar to many high-quality software. Obviously, more people go for bells and whistles and put their bonnet up.

Every passionate driver loves a stick shift, a.k.a. manual gear shift car. Non-passionate ones love the fully automatic ones because they want to do other things while driving the car. Similar to how passionate testers want to test through their hands too, even if there's automation running.

If customers had an app like Uber to see when the release is going to come, they'd see the car come close and then decide to take a big roundabout, take the highway, and then come back to the road they were supposed to board from.

A car that is being driven well can still end up in a crash due to some other car driver's mistake, similar to how a third-party app or SDK integrated can cause the whole app to crash. Assessing the ability to let the passengers (users) recover from it is a key part of testing.

Most products are built with a roadmap, but last-minute features, changes, and scope creep make the product go off-roadmap, similar to how it feels to buy a hatchback and take it off-roading. It will end up needing a tow and a lot of time at the service center eventually.

Most people who know how to drive a car really well can't fix a flat tire, similar to how many developers who write good functional code can't fix a performance issue resulting from their code.

Many people with money to buy a luxury car actually end up buying a mid-tier car because they have the money to buy a super luxury car, but not the money to keep affording its maintenance. Similarly, software is an expensive luxury car that needs more money to maintain over the years than the money required to have built it.

ADAS and cruise control enable people to not hold the steering wheel with the pressure they usually hold, but people misuse it as a fully autonomous solution, similar to how AI is best suited for assisted developing and testing, and people are trying to use it as a fully autonomous solution.

Waymo recently admitted that many of their fully autonomous cars are driven by drivers in the Philippines, watching over and guiding them passively. Unlike most tech companies who claim to be releasing without needing testers, they fail to admit their testing is actually outsourced to an offshore testing partner.

Expecting people to drive without fog lights in foggy conditions, without causing an accident, is like expecting a test team to regression test bug fixes and yet give a stable release, where the architecture is known to have cracks.

Flying

Flying

Unsupervised AI is like the captain and co-pilot taking a leak in the toilets at the same time while the plane is on autopilot. It works well on good weather days, but if we reduce the number of pilots in the cockpit, the business will come crashing down, while no one is there to take over and save it.

Making a trainee pilot supervise autopilot and calling the trainee a captain (because there is an AI co-pilot), while the real captain is absent, is actually putting the trainee's life and others in danger. Similar to how junior developers and testers are risking their careers relying on AI to do things, businesses risk their customers and revenue by letting the juniors build complex production-grade code.

Safety is the number one priority in flying, and rigorous practices are put in place for ground staff, pilots, and cabin crew to prioritize it because a poor safety record dents the business and credibility of an airline. Similarly, those leaders who see quality as a number one priority will find a way to build quality and win the market through quality rather than building it over speed.

An airline with a high rate of on-time arrivals but a poor safety record will eventually lose its business, similar to how a company with frequent feature releases but a poor-quality record will lose its profitability.

The money required to fly comfortably and test comfortably are very similar. Most testers are in economy class budget, very few in business class, and very rarely in first class. Every tester wants to graduate to business class, but it is a luxury they get to experience on a free upgrade or a lot of miles accumulation and redeemed.

When flight time is constantly postponed, the passengers go through frustration, and some of them lose their cool, similar to how when a build to arrive is constantly postponed and arrives at a time when someone's planned leave is starting soon, making them frustrated.

The educated, aware passengers do know that most of the flying of the plane is done by the autopilot, but they are not stressed because the well-trained captain and his co-pilot are there to catch errors of the autopilot and take manual control. Unlike in the software world, decision-makers do want pilotless testing without realizing that bringing in a human after late realization will still not be useful enough because the human brought in lacks the context and history of things that have gone wrong.

Connecting flights to catch with short layovers and a large airport are quite a stressful experience for every traveler, similar to having a reduced timeline to test and more changes to test with a smaller number of people in the team for a test lead.

When traveling economy, meals have to be pre-booked. Expecting a customized meal to be cooked and served by a chef mid-air, like in first class of some airlines, is what many leaders in the software world do, expecting their economy budget test teams.

Traveling with kids takes a lot of extra time to be factored in, similar to releasing a critical piece of software with more juniors on the team.

Most airlines board the senior citizens and passengers with kids first to ease out everyone's onboarding experience, similar to how a good bug triage works by prioritizing the bugs that cause maximum stress to the user, to enhance their experience of continuing to use the software.

Most unruly passengers behave rudely to the ground staff and cabin crew. Very rarely do pilots experience it. Similarly, the support teams and testers take the brunt of frustrated users, and very rarely, the developers.

Cricket

Cricket

In cricket, it takes eleven people to cover the big ground. Fewer can do, too, but there would be more boundaries and catches missed. Too many people covering the ground would make the game boring. Similarly, based on the complexity and test coverage needed, a certain number of testers are required to be a part of a team. Having a lesser number of testers ends up with more observations missed, and more testers make it a boring project to be a tester on.

In cricket, a catch is considered as a miss only if the player puts the hand on the ball and misses it, but in testing - even if the bug is far away, many leadership teams think the tester missed catching the bug.

In cricket, there is just one ball that the whole fielding team is trying to catch, yet they miss it many times. Unlike testing, where bugs are flying all over, and testers are expected to catch all bugs at the same time because there is a test for it somewhere inside the company.

When the ball gets worn out in a test match, a new ball is issued, but in the world of testing, when a test gets obsolete, we still continue to use it.

Cricket is a team sport. The bowler can bowl well, but if the fielders misfield and miss catches, the overall runs scored by the opponent team will grow, and the team loses. In testing, if the people documenting requirements, the people responsible for writing unit tests and integration tests, and the architecture and design teams make a mistake, it will show up as more work in front-end exploratory testing, and that is when the team loses. Less laborious work for front-end testing and less work for support teams means a good job done by all.

Finding bugs in early-stage software products is like batting in the power play. It's easy to not get caught when hitting near the boundary because very few fielders are spread near the boundary. But finding bugs in mature products is like the middle overs. It's tough, requires discipline, and involves picking and choosing when and how to find them.

A bug bash is like a twenty-over format. Being in a project for a long time is like a test match. Those who shine in the twenty-over format may not be able to withstand the long persistence required to field and bat over the extended duration the test match requires.

Working in a sprint as a tester is like playing in one-day matches. The most runs to be scored or scored are in the last five overs. The last ten overs are exciting and nervous times, but the twenty to forty is the hard work period. The first ten overs set the stage for a win or a failure.

In cricket, a team is picked based on a combination of specialists and all-rounders, but in testing, every company and every Job Description (JD) wants everyone to be only an all-rounder.

Most JDs in testing are like: we need someone who can bowl fast, bowl spin, bowl medium pace, bat against swing, bat against spinners, bat in the middle order as well as in the tail end, and hit centuries consistently, and take five wickets in every match with an economy of four or lower.

Are testers like batters or bowlers? Neither. They are wicket keepers and fielders who are also expected to do well in batting or bowling to survive leadership thinking of them as a cost. It takes mastery to field like Jhonty Rhodes or keep like MS Dhoni to be noticed for the skill of fielding and keeping, respectively. Many matches are actually won by fielders and keepers that never get mentioned.

Reviewing the Testing function for many org leaders is like watching a cricket match on television, especially when the team they were supporting lost the match. They have opinions of how people should have played without having the actual skills to do it themselves.

The rules in cricket are reasonable, whereas in testing, it is unreasonable. In cricket, if rains interrupt the play hours, umpires use the Duckworth-Lewis method to reduce the target and overs. In the world of software, if the build is delayed to testers, the leaders expect the same target to be hit in fewer hours than originally planned.

Cricket formats are Test, One Day, and 2020, demanding different kinds of skills, similar to how short-haul, medium-haul, and long-haul tests reveal different bugs and behavior of software. Most tests done by most tools, most humans, and most AI are short-haul - shallow tests. That's why customers end up finding the long-haul - deep value ones.

Cricket has a Third Umpire to enable players to review a decision made by a human, and the third umpire uses tech and slow-mo to review a decision. Many testers wish such a third umpire existed to review bugs that got classified as "Won't fix." The next day, a customer reports the same bug, which then gets classified as "Critical." In some cases, "Why did you not find this?"

Too many series and too many matches played by a team before a World Cup fatigue the team and put them out of form, similar to how testers get fatigued by too many releases before a demanding major release.

Every cricket team has a substitute who comes in handy when a player gets injured or falls sick in between a series, unlike most test teams, who have zero substitutes, and most testers end up being their own substitute.

Many great batsmen and bowlers can substitute in fielding and do well, but cannot substitute in wicket-keeping, similar to how many software developers and leaders can write code, but cannot test.

Wicket-keeping in cricket and being a goalkeeper in football are unique skills within the sport, similar to how testing is unique within product and engineering. A player cannot just double up and do a good job. An average job, absolutely.

Formula 1

Formula 1

Last-minute bug fixing and releases are like trying to fix a car that hit the barriers in the formation lap and caused the race to be red-flagged. The expectation from such fixes, even if they work, should not be to win the race but, at best, to finish the race without the race leader lapping twice.

Testing in a staging environment and qualifying a build to release is like setting a P1 in qualifying and hoping it would convert to P1 on race day as well. The race pace and qualifying pace are often different, and equally, race day has different weather conditions that affect the tire degradation that was not seen in free practice or qualifying. Free Practice and Qualifying are hypotheses only.

A Formula 1 car has super automation built inside it, with a human expert at the driving wheel. The testing world forgets the human expert and aims to achieve an F1 car driven without the human expert.

Even a winning car on a wrong tire strategy will fail to get a podium result, similar to how a skilled team on a wrong test strategy will fail to achieve necessary test coverage.

The qualifying pace and race pace aren't necessarily the same because the race day has a different weather condition, dirty air flow to deal with while overtaking, and having to conserve tires. Similarly, the way code works in a staging environment and production environment has a huge variance in most organizations because the environment variables are different, the amount of data stored and processed is different, and of course, the load.

Many races are won by the combination of a super driver in a super car who got a great pit stop because of the pit crew doing a super job, but never once is the pit crew celebrated as the 33% contributing factor for that day's win. Testers expecting an award for a great release is similar to the pit crew claiming to have made a champion possible. True, but there's no trophy for that.

Formula 1 is a technology-heavy sport, like testing software. While the tech pulls the crowd in F1, the human drivers get celebrated, unlike in Testing. In testing, the humans that are celebrated are those who throw more tech at Testing.

Formula 1 is like testing. A boring thing to many who think, "Why are fast cars going around in circles around the circuit, and what's the point?" Only those who are deep into it notice the nuances and enjoy it so much that they are soaked in ecstasy while on it.

Like Formula 1, some releases are on rainy days, where the situation is slippery, and sometimes champions make mistakes, and rookies win. Leaders who don't take cognizance of the slippery situations and just keep pushing for ideal condition release are just satisfying their ego.

Some cars are designed to be more suitable for higher downforce circuits, and other cars are more suited for straight-line speeds, just like how some testers are suited for tricky situations and some are suited for straightforward testing needs. It becomes the leader's role in choosing who leads in what type of condition.

Just like Formula 1, some teams have two equally good competitive testers fighting against each other and denting the team's possibilities. Bringing two equally talented people together needs a strong culture of how people respect each other, that most often IT companies overlook.

The best pit stop recorded in Formula 1 is 1.8 seconds, and three seconds is considered a slow pit stop. A blink of an eye to remove four wheels and fit in new ones. To be able to achieve this, teams practice a hundred thousand times. In the software world, 99% of people do zero practice outside of work, and their workplace becomes a practice zone. So obviously, many mistakes creep in.

Every few years, like how Formula 1 goes through a full change in regulations to the engine, fuel, and design, software engineering also goes through those changes due to tech and process revolutions. Organizations that let go of their testers who held domain and customer knowledge prior to such a revolutionary change struggle to cope with the new change.

Formula 1 drivers who push their cars to over 300 km/h on race circuits drive their cars slowly and as per speed regulations on regular roads because they know that the right environment is required to go fast. However, teen kids of rich parents are known to cause accidents on regular roads trying to push their cars in environments not suitable for those speeds. Most companies' engineering practices aren't suited for rapid release cycles, but they push it because there's fun in it, and cause some permanent damage through tech debt and nasty bugs.

A driver like Lewis Hamilton can be a seven-time world champion and still fail in the first year at Ferrari due to the car and environment. Similarly, when a company with a lot of money hires a great tester but has a poor culture, they are setting up the great tester for failure. Equally, testers who choose an employer purely based on their compensation, without the skill to study if they can succeed in that environment, could also be setting themselves up for failure.

Table Tennis

Table Tennis

"Feeling" is a word most commonly used in modern-day table tennis. It is considered to be a top skill because it is the ability of the player to sense the spin coming in toward them, just like how very few testers on this planet have a "feeling" that a specific type of bug is going to walk toward them based on a code change being planned.

For a long time, table tennis was a boring sport to watch, just like how testing was boring to do and watch someone test, but table tennis got modernized, and testing still remains boring to many.

Football is fun to watch, so more kids want to sign up for it than play table tennis. Similar to how development is hyped to be more exciting than testing, more kids want to become a developer than a tester, although football and table tennis are equal in fun and challenge.

The last ten Olympics gold in Table Tennis have gone to Chinese players because they have a strong academy right from childhood for kids to lay a strong foundation, unlike testing where the academy is weak all across the globe, and hence most testers think shallow and develop slowly in their career.

There are two goals that every table tennis player tries hard to achieve when they are receiving the ball from an opponent. One, put the ball back in the opponent's court, and two, to put it in a way that scores a point. Putting the ball back in the opponent's court sounds like a functionality pass in testing, and winning sounds like value to the customer. Most companies just want to make a functionality work rather than win the customer because of the functionality.

Coaches get a player trained with multiball, which is feeding several balls for the player to practice hitting a shot continuously. There's a robot now that feeds the ball, but the Table Tennis sport hasn't replaced the role of a coach, unlike in Testing. People think now that there's automation - let's replace those who were doing it. The smallest part of what the coach was doing is to feed balls, but the coach had the eyes on how the player is responding to provide feedback and course correct the shot to near perfection. Not all testers observe and know how to articulate the feedback, but even they get replaced in the name of automation (and now AI).

Practice in table tennis appears like a lot of repetition. Trying to play the same topspin over and over and over again. Unless someone is passionate, they won't enjoy so much repetition, and that repetition is similar to testing that truly has a lot of repetitiveness to the work to be able to get to excellence.

Muscle memory is everything in table tennis, because when the ball is blazing through, sometimes at 80 km/h toward the player, they have no time to think and react. Most companies get their testers to build muscle memory to test within a sprint, and hence, these testers don't know how to test end-to-end because they have no muscle memory of it.

Footwork is invisible in the sport of table tennis - the camera and people see the ball and the player's upper body, while the success is determined by the footwork, similar to how the success of testing and automation is determined by testability that no one notices and cares about. No wonder most testing and automation fails.

Someone who has played against an inverted rubber will fail the moment they play against pips, irrespective of how good their game is, similar to how testers used to a certain approach of testing will fail the moment the complexity or context has changed.

Context is like a ball in a table tennis match - the direction and position are constantly being changed by someone, but in table tennis, the context change is visible. In the software world, it is invisible, forcing the skill of finding the context to be the most needed one in testing, but the most ignored one.

When a topspin ball is returned in an inverted rubber, hard rubber, tacky rubber, anti-rubber, short pips, medium pips, and long pips, it comes back very differently, similar to how software behaves differently for different inputs. Only sufficient time to test and sufficient tests reveal its holistic behavior. Today, most people qualify software based on hitting it against one or two kinds of rubber, but customers have all sorts of rubbers.

A table tennis player and a tester are both focused on coverage. One on the coverage of the ball on a table, and the other on the tests in the software. Interestingly, the table is not expanding, but the software is constantly expanding.

In most sports, like table tennis, top champions retire from active play after a certain time and become a coach, enabling others to become a champion. Unlike in software, they become managers and don't coach people to succeed.

Table tennis is a precision sport. It requires too many things to align to be able to send the ball back to the opponent's court, similar to testing - only a precise test reveals a certain bug. Some bugs become irreproducible because people have not built the software with the testability to control and test with precision.

A player in a match feels bad for missing a ball in play, but moves on to the next point, unlike some delusional and passionate testers who go to bed thinking why they missed a bug.

Most people seem great at table tennis while they are practicing counter rallies during warm-up, but can't take it to the third rally point in the game, similar to how some people in the software world look so good on their profile and interview but fail on the job.

The blade and rubber certainly help people to play well to a certain minimal degree only; beyond that, it is human skill that helps a player win a match, just like testing tools don't change the outcome of a project unless human skill is sufficiently available and a conducive environment exists.

There are players with the same blade and rubber as the world champion, yet don't qualify for the knockouts. This is similar to how many companies have invested more in tools and less in people, thinking they can win like other champion companies because they have the same tools.

The job of a sports coach is to teach the form, techniques, and train for muscle memory, and help improve the skill, but most importantly, reaffirm a good thing the player is doing naturally or on their own to bring tremendous amounts of confidence. Similarly, the role of a test coach is that of teaching approaches, techniques, enabling skill-building through exercises, and importantly, highlighting what the tester is doing naturally well.

The joy and high a player gets by winning a point, hitting a backhand topspin from far off the table, is similar to the joy a tester gets in finding a critical bug that existed in the system for a long time, and no one in the past could find or credibly report it to get it fixed.

Fishing

Fishing

Knowing which bug to find is important to decide what type of tests to run. Just like in fishing, knowing which fish one intends to catch determines their choice of lure and bait. Yes, sometimes when one is retrieving a small fish, a big fish chases that and bites onto it. That's just pure luck, and only anglers know that type of luck is one in half a million casts. That cannot be a strategy.

Poor test coverage leads to fewer areas explored and fewer bugs found. A successful angler casts in all different directions despite having caught a fish in one direction because fishes move, and they can be anywhere at any given point in time. Only when an area is sufficiently covered and given sufficient time is an angler able to move on from that place, feeling content that the area is covered.

Catching small fishes can become addictive if they are especially easy to catch, similar to catching bugs that aren't going to be too high on priority to fix. The big ones that matter to be caught are harder to catch and need a bit more risk-taking from the angler.

Some fish that are not endemic to that place should not be released once caught, because they are invasive, similar to how some bugs must be fixed once reported. Otherwise, they multiply and end up with never-ending regression bugs to the point that being a software engineer on that project sucks.

Sometimes fishing is not about catching – it is about being in the lap of nature and enjoying the calmness. Similarly, testing isn't about catching bugs alone – it is about being there and experiencing what customers would experience, and assessing if it is beautiful enough for them to pay.

Finding bugs, like catching a fish, is also about timing. Certain types of fishes are active during certain times and certain tides only. If that timing is missed and a thousand casts are made, the result will be zero.

Just because there were no fish caught, an angler cannot ascertain that the waters don't have fishes. Similarly, just because a team is unable to find bugs anymore, doesn't mean there are no bugs lurking over there.

Being passionate about fishing and testing works similarly. It either wakes someone up very early or makes them stay up late and continue to do the same thing over and over again without needing instant gratification.

The strength of the knot is similar to the strength of a test. The disappointment of an angler is very high when a large fish that was hooked managed to escape because the knot wasn't strong enough. Bugs get hooked, but become irreproducible sometimes because the test wasn't strong enough to isolate the bug from the product behavior.

A snag to a newbie angler feels like a strike from a fish. The newbies reel faster the moment they hit a snag, in an excitement that they caught a fish, making the lure unretrievable. Similarly, newbie testers report a small observation they found as a major breakthrough and, repeatedly doing it, dents their credibility with the team.

Changing lures is essential to bring in a variation to attract and catch a fish. Similarly, changing tests is essential to catch a bug. Sometimes a particular bug responds to different tests in a different way.

Many unsuccessful casts have had a fish that came close, but didn't bite. Similarly, many tests have had a bug come close to being found, but the test was close, but not close enough to make the bug discoverable.

Fishes migrate - so do bugs. If they are at one spot today, they might be at another spot tomorrow. Knowing where they lurk takes experience to find out. Repeating the same tests at the same place isn't always helpful. Every release should have new tests in addition to old tests, hitting the same place in a different way or different places than what were being hit.

Pairing up with an expert angler short-circuits years of learning, similar to how pair testing with an expert tester fast-forwards our learning by several months.

The setup to catch a fish is critical to also land it successfully. If the drag on the reel is set up too tight, the fish can break the line more easily. Similarly, the test setup matters to landing a bug successfully. Ninety percent of the bugs escape despite the test being right, and the setup to land them was wrong.

Sometimes an angler has to cast at certain places where there is a thin line between getting snagged and hooking a big fish. Expert anglers take the chance, just like how expert testers take the chance to run an overnight test. The system might hang, or in the morning, a big bug awaits being reported.

Technologies like Fish Finder are helpful when time is a constraint and money is available, but still don't guarantee the fish will bite. Similarly, bringing more tools requires more budgets and more time investment from people, but still doesn't guarantee good test coverage. It is the expert that brings more value than the tools do. The tool multiplies the value of the expert. Without the expert, the tool by itself is useless.

Junior testers are like a braided line. Good for a lot of hard work, but still, you need a leader (line) to prevent the braid from getting cut off when fishing in rocky areas (tough, complex scenarios). A good leader line keeps the fish thinking the lure is real and takes the shock, preventing the braid from getting cut off.

Landing a large fish is always very challenging. Just because it is hooked, it doesn't mean it can be landed, as large fish have the power to cut off the line or even bend the hook, similar to how some critical but intermittent bugs are. They get hooked once in a while, but to land them requires the skill to isolate and find that one variable causing it.

Some anglers are experts at taking pictures of the fish they caught, making it look bigger than it actually is, similar to how some testers are experts at making a bug look more critical than it truly is.

A bug bash is like casting a large net to catch fish - all sorts of fish will get caught in it, and filtering them for a specific fish can become hard.

A nice fishing spot is often kept a secret by an angler until one becomes their friend. Similarly, some cool bug-finding approaches and areas within the software are kept hidden from a tester by their colleagues unless they pair test and learn it tacitly.

Lego

Lego

It requires a high level of mastery and understanding of users for someone to have written the Lego instructions kit, similar to how someone should possess a great mastery to write test scenarios when it involves a high complexity of setup.

Building Lego through hands is a way to build skills, learn troubleshooting, make observations, and develop patience, similar to how testing by hand yields what the modern generation bypasses with automation or AI.

Different Lego blocks are different pieces of code that have to fit together tightly as the whole software is built; otherwise, one small pressure at a wrong angle while integrating two large components can make the whole software break down.

The joy of building a Lego set is in every step of building it, and so should be in building different components of the software. However, the reality in most companies is that people want to forget the sprint that just ended.

Testing and debugging Lego requires visual inspection, knowing what it should look like as an end product, and going back to the instructions kit. Unlike in software, most people testing and debugging have no clue what the end product should look like for users.

In Lego, people pay money to rebuild the product, unlike in software, where people are paying money with the hope that the software doesn't need to be rebuilt to actually meet its purpose.

Following the Lego instruction kit manual for a 40+ year-old person with presbyopia and without prescription glasses is as difficult as a junior tester who is asked to follow a complex test script to mark a test as pass or fail.

Every software is a Lego set for a software tester. The curious ones learn it faster, and the ones obligated to do it feel the Lego lacks joy. Lego is joy!

The more Lego sets one builds, they understand the next one faster, similar to how those who have seen a variety of software understand the next one faster.

The people who build a Lego set without reading instructions are doing it for the joy of it, similar to how some testers testing the software without needing documented test cases are doing it for the joy of it.

People in their twenties take less than half the time to build the same Lego set compared to a forty-five-year-old, because the forty-five-year-old is programmed to think critically. There's value in twenty-year-olds and forty-five-year-olds doing testing. The forty-five-year-olds think critically, and the twenty-year-olds aid speed. A good test team often needs people who move fast and people who think critically. However, the IT industry is mostly wired for speed.

Instagram

Instagram

Testing plenty of releases of the same product with similar bug fixes is like watching the same dance reel danced by different people. Same song, same steps, and different people, and after a while, we just swipe because we are too bored.

Scrolling the reels with the thumb is the most repetitive thing that automation engineers in testing do in real life, without automating it, because it is exciting to do it (or they lack a testability layer to do it). When it's fun to do, it will be done manually, even by people who think "all repetitive actions need to be automated."

Every time we flip, we get a new reel with a new, irrelevant context to what we saw previously, but also the pattern repeats itself after watching a few reels - much like what happens while being online on Slack or Teams. The context keeps changing, and the mind doesn't know which one to focus on, but on a zoomed-out view, everyone is talking about the same problem.

Creating an original reel that is liked by many is hard, so many people just copy a trend to get likes, just like how creating original test cases is hard, and testers end up copying test cases that have been written a thousand times by thousands of people for similar features. This is why AI is becoming exciting in testing because it is the best copycat in the world.

Not every person on Instagram who has a large number of followers is an influencer. Similarly, not every software that has a high pass percentage in tests is high-quality software.

Instagram influencers have made some tourist places horrible by creating large crowds of people queuing up to get that one magical photo, similar to how people obsessed with heavily scripted test cases spoil testing for exploratory testers.

Instagram reel and dance trends keep changing, as test-automation tool trends change. Every influencer wants to keep moving to new trends to keep their audience engaged, and every automation engineer keeps updating their profile with new trending tools to keep themselves employable.

95% of users of Instagram don't publish anything; they just consume what is published, similar to how 95% of testers don't think and test; they just blindly follow test cases or automate test cases without assessing their usefulness.

WhatsApp and Instagram are interlinked by Meta to provide contextual ads to people. If someone had a discussion about a knee on WhatsApp, Instagram starts showing ads of knee braces and wheelchairs. This is similar to how many people treat their requirement documents and test cases. Every line of a requirement document is treated as an expected result in the test cases and is expected to fulfill the criteria of test coverage.

Doctors, nurses, teachers, and surgeons, who can also dance and make reels, are more influential in modern-day society than their colleagues who are equally good in their profession but don't know how to dance. Similarly, testers who know how to speak, write, and present themselves well are more influential than their colleagues who are equal in testing skills but are in the previous era, thinking that their work should do the speaking for them.

The attention span of people scrolling on Instagram is getting shorter and shorter by the day, and people are switching context too fast, similar to how the tests are becoming shallower by the day because people are switching between contexts too fast.

By doing more reels that appear to get likes, many influencers lose their identity, similar to how many software companies lose their USP by releasing more features customers can be forced to pay for.

More and more people doom-scroll on Instagram - their attention span goes lower and lower by the day. Similarly, more and more people who generate and accept test cases using AI that start with "verify if x works" - their depth of testing goes shallower by the day.

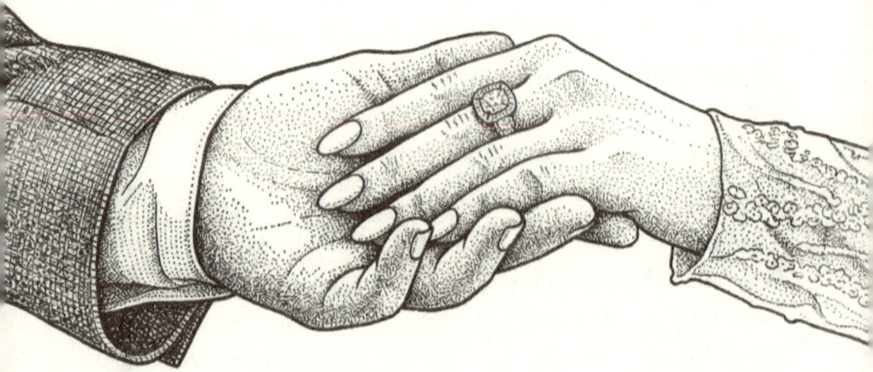

Dating & Married Life

Dating and Married Life

Software and married life are very similar. There can never be a perfect one, but they can be made good enough with care, empathy, and support over time.

A homemaker's job is the hardest in the world, and that is perhaps why some people think testing is a job any homemaker can do (and the people saying it can't).

Sometimes a tester's life is similar to an eighties-era wife. Does a lot of hard work, brings empathy, goes through labor pain, handles multiple stakeholders, brings the balance, gets the least credit, gets taken for granted, and compensated least.

A marriage that looked very successful from the outside can break at any moment in an unpredictable fashion, like how a software that worked consistently over the years can break down overnight. A strong support system is required in such cases.

When a couple is working hard to make ends meet and, in parallel, produce more and more kids, their life strains very deeply, similar to how an already buggy software adding more features to it strains the software and people working on it very deeply.

In some cultures, a happy married life is constantly disturbed and negatively influenced by relatives and in-laws, similar to how a good software can be troubled by buggy third-party plug-ins and SDKs and made to look buggy for its customers.

Jokes made about married life, husband, and wife are funny, not necessarily real all the time and are shareworthy between happy couples, similar to how jokes made about developers and testers are shareworthy between a good partnership of dev and test.

In some cultures, people spend a lot of money for the marriage event, and then the couple struggles to earn that money back, similar to how some companies spend a lot of money on tools and parties and very little investment to train people, making people struggle to get work done.

Some people who are good at dating may not be good at being a partner, similar to how some people who are good at interviewing may not be good at working at that company.

Some people find it difficult to speak on their first date, but are very chatty once they build a comfort zone, similar to how some apps are designed to be good to use on a daily basis, but it is a struggle to get onboarded into it.

In a dating app, most men swipe most women's pics right with a hope to find a match, and women carefully choose whom to swipe right. Similarly, people who do not understand testing swipe all test cases right in a hope to achieve test coverage, and those who know testing are careful which tests to retain and which to swipe left, and when to achieve good enough test coverage.

Dating in the future is going to be AI presenting a set of pre-screened prospects based on the person's online activity, and yes, it sounds as weird as the future of testing in some people's vision, that a set of agents will generate requirements, generate code, test it, and deploy it.

Dating apps act like a testability layer. It enables people - otherwise shy - to get connected online and go on in-person dates. Without testability, many good people would remain single for long.

Dating is a shallow test before deciding to live with someone for a long time, similar to how automated tests are shallow and act as a qualifying factor for humans to test.

Some people are good on the first date and bad on the second, similar to how some software is good at First Time User Experience and bad for subsequent use.

In some cultures, there is plenty of conflict between mother-in-law and daughter-in-law post-marriage about the control of the house. The husband takes a lot of hits because he can't side with either, similar to how when engineering and product leaders conflict, the tester plays the husband.

Most of the time, the wife remembers things the husband said that the husband forgot themselves, similar to how most of the time the testers remember the bugs that they warned will affect the customer, and the leaders who decided not to fix the bug during triage forget that the tester raised it but ask the tester why they did not report the bug just after they heard a customer complain about it.

No marriages exist without friction, but the ones that survive and blossom harmoniously despite the friction have both the husband and wife having a common goal toward living life peacefully. Similarly, no organization can exist without business, development, product, and testing having some level of friction, but the ones that do well all align to the vision of the company, making their conflicts incidental to caring for customers.

Living with someone and marrying the same person can look similar, but can change the relationship dynamics post-marriage, similar to testing the software and using the software can bring a different dynamic altogether in how someone experiences the software.

How does one deal with a breakup is only known when they are dealing with one. Similar to how a leader deals with an escalation, can only be known after the escalation and not during an interview or a regular working day.

Breakups in relationships during dating and marriage are becoming more common than they were, giving rise to an increase in counsellors and attorneys who specialize in resolving conflicts. This is similar to how in some organizations, the regression issues due to accumulated tech debt are growing at a high rate, leading to the need for more and more testers to test.

A couple gets married, accumulates debt, and brings multiple children into this world. They struggle throughout their lifetime clearing debt, similar to how founders build too fast, too poorly, and accumulate a tech debt that they keep serving over the years, tiring their lives and those of their teams.

It requires a different skill and mindset to make long-distance relationships work well, similar to how it requires a different skillset and mindset of leaders to make outsourced and offshore testing work well, which most of them don't have.

Parenting

Parenting

Bringing a child to this Earth may take nine months, but enabling the child to become a good human takes decades, similar to how putting a software with minimal functional usage is easy, but building quality into it is a long and continuous process.

In some cultures, a father celebrates his child's birth but doesn't participate in cleaning the poop and changing diapers, similar to how some software organization cultures have developers take pride in writing code but aren't willing to test and clean their own mess.

A toddler is more likely to fall sick because the immunity building is still happening within their body, similar to how early-stage software is likely to have plenty of bugs while the processes of quality are still evolving within the team.

Every parent would be disappointed if, when given a toy, their kid asks for an instruction manual to play with it, but the same parents, at work as leaders of their org, want grown adults to follow test cases with step-by-step instructions to test software.

A software is a forever toddler. Like how a toddler stands up, falls, stands up again, building quality is a continuous process where there shall be a fall sometimes, and the team has to stand up and put things together to make it happen when something falls.

Giving slack and teams to people working together on the same floor is like giving teenage kids smartphones. They'd sit and chat over the phone and interact very little in person.

Kids love pets, and when they bring one home, the responsibility to nurture the pet falls on parents, similar to how some leaders love to bring some consultants into the company, who become a responsibility of people on the ground to deal with. Leaders feel they have done a great job.

The stress of parenting sometimes overshadows the joy of parenting, similar to how the stress of building quality overshadows the joy of customer experience.

When the second kid arrives, parents bring all the wisdom they had with their first, only to discover that the second kid has rewritten the rules of parenting, similar to how when experienced team members arrive on a new project, they bring all their learning, and then an unknown variable resets their learning.

Kids mimic their parents, learn the language they are speaking, and the body language, similar to how junior testers mimic the seniors and leaders in an org.

When two kids fight with each other, parents always become unpopular with one of them by giving their perspective of who is right and wrong, similar to how testers become unpopular when Product and Engineering are not aligned, and they have to agree with one and disagree with another.

People who care for the quality of software in an organization are like breastfeeding mothers. They are tired, sleep-deprived, going through postpartum, and yet nourishing the baby to grow.

Homeschooling a child is a very high responsibility toward parents, and most parents don't have the patience, skills, and time to focus on their child. Hence, schools succeed, similar to how building a test team is a great responsibility that most companies don't have the focus toward (because the focus is on building other teams). Therefore, testing is one of the most outsourced activities in the engineering lifecycle, while building development teams mostly happens internally.

Schools don't replace parenting, and some parents are disappointed to learn that despite paying a lot of fees, they still have to work with their kids, similar to how many companies who outsource their testing think that they no longer have anything to do with quality and are disappointed to know that quality is still a joint responsibility.

Good parenting is about becoming good friends with kids, allowing them to open up and talk about any topic, much like the culture of high-quality treats testers as good friends, enabling them to speak up against a decision if necessary, and not forcing a sign-off.

Giving a smartphone as a primary toy to a toddler is as bad as giving AI to a junior programmer and a tester. It spoils the mind from further developing, and the attitude the world carries is; but who cares - let us do whatever is required for solving today's problem.

Parents in India, back in the eighties and nineties, hardly changed the school for their kids unless they relocated to another city, but today, a growing population of parents, despite living in the same city, change schools for the kids two to three times before reaching twelfth grade because of choices and FOMO. This is similar to how many companies used to stick to one automation framework in the past, but today keep changing their automation framework before it starts to yield results and value.

Modern-day parental care is all about moderating what kids do consume over the internet, and less of what kids do in person, similar to how modern-day testing is all about focusing on what goes into automation than what goes in human-aided exploratory testing.

Release decisions in most organizations that require a sign-off from testers. When testers say no, the decision-makers behave like kids who get a no from Mom. They go to Dad and get a yes, then say, "Dad said yes, so I went ahead."

When a kid is being given a toy or allowed to play, they are happy, and they get cranky when the toy is taken away or playtime is being cut, similar to how most software behaves quite well for happy path scenarios and suddenly becomes buggy when there's a deviation from the happy path.

Loving the kid and being strict with the kid needs to be balanced, yet most parents get it wrong, where they either give too much love and too little strictness, or vice versa, similar to how testers should find a balance between saying No and saying Yes to what decision-makers want to do with software that affects quality.

Parents celebrate their children's success and take their children's failure as their personal failure, similar to how some passionate testers in the software industry take software success and failure personally.

Kids are the legacy parents leave behind, and some of them turn out good, while a few turn out bad, similar to how developers leave behind code as their legacy. Some turn out to be features, and some turn out to be bugs.

Most teens in the modern age get super irritated to hear from their mother that they should clean their own rooms, even when it is super messy, similar to how some leaders get irritated to hear from testers that the bugs are coming from requirements, last-minute scope creeps, and unplanned patch releases, and not from coding and testing.

The process of school and college admission is a stressful and anxious phase for both parents and kids, similar to how a regulatory audit of a software is for testers and leaders of an org.

When a mother and daughter are fighting, the father goes in to resolve the conflict, and when the father and son are fighting, the mother goes in to resolve the conflict, similar to how when test and dev are fighting, the product steps in to resolve the issue, and when product and engineering are fighting, leadership steps in to resolve the issue.

Impatient parents are likely to create impatient kids, similar to how impatient leaders create impatient engineers.

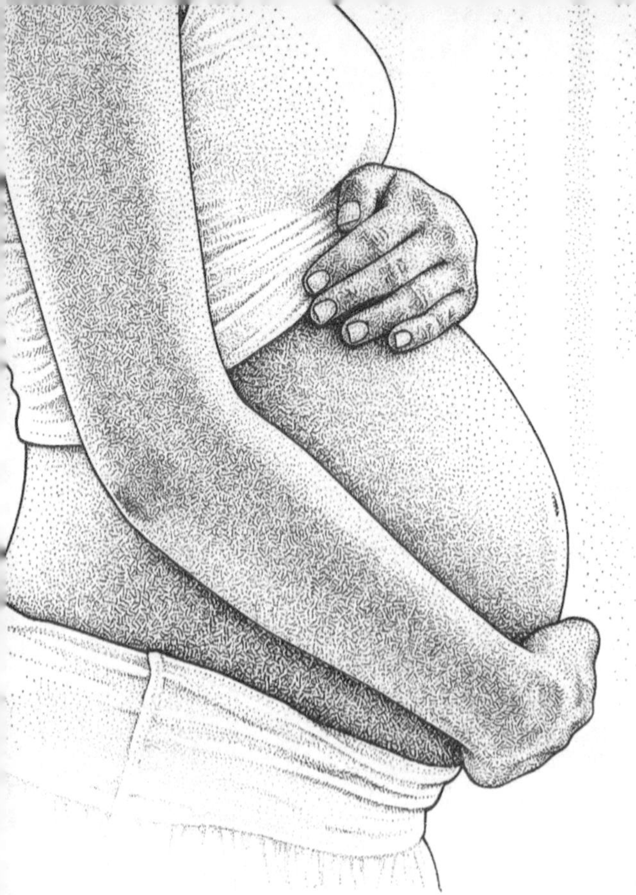

Menstruation, Pregnancy & Menopause

Menstruation, Pregnancy and Menopause

Menstruation is a time frame of cramps, pain, and blood loss, similar to how the last few days prior to release are for many testers in companies where there is no culture of dev notes and unit testing.

Menstruation is the natural process of removal of an unused and worn-out part of the ecosystem inside the body to make way for the new, fresh one to be born. Unlike in the software world, humans go against nature and don't remove the wasted features. Instead, they keep adding more wasteful features on top of useless features, corrupting the software quality and making it incredibly hard to test and use.

When a period that is supposed to come at a certain time fails to come, the pain of it is similar to that of a build expected to come on Thursday afternoon for testing being postponed to Friday evening.

A woman's feeling of going through a menstruation cycle every month is something a man can never fully understand, similar to how the pain testers go through to navigate through multiple stakeholders' expectations in every release, the management can never understand.

False positive and false negative pregnancy test results are the most troublesome ones that have a lot of emotional turmoil on a woman, similar to how a false positive or a false negative test result has on the person who wrote the automation script when decisions made based on pass/fail go wrong.

Self-test pregnancy test kits are like surface-level tests and a pre-condition test to a proper blood test and scan for deeper analysis to prevent complications, and not a replacement for it. Similarly, automated checks are pre-tests to human-driven testing and not a replacement for it.

Scans at regular intervals are essential during the pregnancy phase to monitor the health of both the mother and baby, to take corrective action at the appropriate time, similar to how testing software regularly shows not just the software's health but also the professional health of the people.

Medicine that enables a period cycle to be skipped causes more damage to the body than a woman could have comprehended before taking it, similar to how a decision to not fix a certain bug can have huge ramifications on the quality of the software, and the leaders couldn't have comprehended it.

Sometimes, women cry because they got their periods, and sometimes they cry because they did not. This is similar to how testers sometimes feel good that the build didn't arrive, and they feel bad that the build did arrive.

A woman going through perimenopause goes through hot flashes, which is a very annoying phase, similar to how some companies release many hotfixes back-to-back, causing frustration and pain to testers on the project.

A woman going through perimenopause goes through sudden hormonal fluctuations, similar to how test managers, who cater to multiple stakeholders pressing panic buttons, go through fluctuations in decisions at different times, and the most affected are the reports of the manager.

Fertility clinics focused on revenue goals try to push a woman toward IVF treatments early in the cycle, similar to how some people push the agenda of automation early in the cycle when the software isn't ready with stability and testability.

Fertility clinics are targeted at women and not men because the businesses understand who is the most vulnerable in the equation. Similarly, feedback on quality is targeted at testers mostly because they are the most vulnerable in the equation.

Traditionally, in some countries and cultures, problems in getting pregnant are usually pinned on a woman's health and body more than a man's, similar to how in some companies, a bug in production is pinned to a tester's primary fault, and everyone else acts secondary to it.

A woman who has to fight through multiple personal and professional priorities while also fighting through her menopause phase goes through very tough times, as much as a test team goes through when business is pushing the software on one side, product is pulling the software on the other side, while the engineering head is trying to move in a total tangential direction, and just when this wasn't sufficient - customers raise escalations.

A woman who arrives at perimenopause in good health, having worked out regularly and with sufficient self-care routines, navigates through perimenopause stronger than a woman who has selflessly cared for others and prioritized herself. Similarly, test teams who push their agenda of testability into the software as much as enabling others' agenda, perform well during a re-architecture of the product compared to the test team who never put their agenda into the software.

Some countries allow their citizens to scan and find the gender of the baby in the womb, while other countries strictly ban knowing the gender, similar to how some companies want testers and developers to collaborate better, and other companies prevent this collaboration, thinking there will be adjustments between them.

Different states in the United States of America have different abortion laws, making it legal in some states and illegal in others, similar to how different teams inside a large company have different test practices, where unit testing is mandatory in some and unit testing appears forbidden in others.

Pets

Pets

Most people find it hard to say no to a cute pet and often give them treats, making the pet's health poor, similar to how testers, saying Yes to things they should not, makes the software quality poor.

Dogs and cats as pets differ in many ways. The dog welcomes the owner when they come home, and the cat expects the owner to come and serve them, similar to how there are organizations who welcome what the tester says and organizations who feel testers are there just to serve them and they don't need to be pleased.

All pets come with a lot of maintenance, and only a few of them will have very little maintenance, similar to how most test-automation solutions come with heavy maintenance costs and very few with low maintenance.

Having a pet is a lot of joy, as long as someone takes up the responsibility of cleaning up after them. Similarly, building a software product is a lot of joy only if someone takes the responsibility of cleaning up after them, and that responsibility largely lies on the testers and developers in bug fix and support roles in most companies.

The larger the dog, the more walk time, play time, and exercise time they need. Otherwise, they become aggressive. Similarly, the larger the software, the more test time and tests it needs in production. Otherwise, it becomes too buggy for people to enjoy working with it.

Once a pet owner falls in love with their pet, and they tolerate the pet's bad behavior a lot, new people coming into the house are surprised at how tolerant they are, similar to how new testers joining an ongoing project find more bugs at the start because their tolerance level is very low compared to people seasoned in the project.

Pet owners' travel and vacation decisions are usually factored in keeping the pet in mind. Similarly, once test automation is in place, a lot of testing decisions are factored around the automation in place. Both of which can be limiting if they want to travel with their pet because not all places welcome pets.

Having a pet at home is an extra cleaning effort responsibility - those who don't like to clean should never have a pet. Similarly, building software comes with a large testing responsibility, and people who don't like testing should ideally not build a product.

Different pets of the same type have different tastes and likings, so they need to be treated differently. Similarly, organizations building different product lines need different approaches to testing, not a universal approach.

Dog owners who take their dogs for a walk get a side-effect health benefit of doing walks, similar to how people who test regularly get a side effect of learning about their product behavior more and more.

Pets repeat a behavior they are taught to, repeatedly, similar to how some testers repeat a certain way of using and testing software, having executed the same script for a while, even though new paths opened up.

There are largely two kinds of classification of people on this Earth: those who like pets and those who dislike them, similar to how people on this Earth can largely be classified as those who like humans testing their software and those who don't.

Having a bird as a pet can sound cruel on them, because they are caged mostly until one realizes that they were not born in the wild and cannot survive in the wild. Similarly, testers whose first few jobs involved shallow testing practices can only survive with shallow practices, and freedom from scripts sounds scary to them.

Untrained dogs pull the owner where it wants to go during a walk, whereas a trained dog goes where the owner wants to take the dog. Similarly, a good quality software follows where the user wants to go, and poor-quality software takes the user where it wants the user to go.

Cats and dogs co-exist harmoniously at several homes, giving a peaceful best of both worlds to pet owners, similar to how testers and developers can co-exist harmoniously too, giving peace and stability to software and its product owners.

Fish are the least intrusive, less everyday maintenance pets that most people keep in their homes. But when the tank cleaning day comes, it requires a lot of work. Similarly, as long as automated tests are green, people keep running them until one day they find some of them are false positives, and a mega cleanup drive begins.

Pets at home demand constant attention, care and nurturing. When taken good care of, they are a joy to be with, always filling us with love; otherwise, constant visits to the vet take away the joy of having a pet. Similarly, building software is like having a pet at home - it needs constant care and nurturing to experience the joy of having built it; otherwise, the regression testing cost grows, and the joy of building it is lost.

Adopting a pet that has been treated badly and behaves very aggressively because of post-traumatic stress disorder is similar in experience to joining a company that has had previous employees screw up the quality of software to a near-irreparable point.

Putting down a terminally ill pet is the hardest decision in one's life, and people fear it similar to how automation engineers treat their obsolete flaky tests and keep them alive.

Air Crash Investigation

Air Crash Investigation

Before the actual official report of an air crash investigation comes out, some sections of the media start blaming the pilot and human error, similar to how when there's a bug in production, some managers already start blaming the tester for missing it out, even before Root Cause Analysis is done to find out what truly happened.

Blackbox plays a critical role in air crash investigation, and a blackbox contains a lot of instrumentation, similar to how the role of testability and logging plays a critical role in bug investigation. Many organizations in the software world don't have time to build testability because a plane can, of course, fly without a blackbox too.

Just because one model of Boeing plane has a high safety record, it doesn't mean anything else Boeing produces as an advanced version will have the same safety record. An upgraded 737 MAX had many crashes before it was grounded due to a software error. Similarly, one new bad release on an existing high-quality software product is all that is required for the quality to significantly drop, making quality a continuous activity. Most people lack continuity.

For a plane to crash, there are a series of things that have to go wrong because it has too many moving parts, and one bolt missing can compound and put an engine on fire. Similarly, for a complex product with too many moving parts - each component quality and their integration matters as to how the whole software holds up.

Building an aircraft requires a lot of documentation work that people are willing to do because it matters to lives. In the software world, people don't want to do documentation because they think it doesn't matter to people's lives. It does.

When there's an engine on fire mid-air, the captain turns off that engine and goes to the checklist or a manual that guides them systematically to land the plane safely with another engine. But in the software world, some leaders already start behaving like the plane has crashed when they see a bug in production.

Some flight crashes are attributed to the pilot believing what the instrumentation or autopilot informed the pilot to do, similar to how the world post-AI looks because people are looking up to AI, telling them what AI did because people building AI wanted to provide visibility to enable supervision.

Boeing CEO was fired due to 737 Max fatal crashes, due to software bugs, because the culture of safety Boeing practiced was overridden by the culture to make more money faster, unlike software company CEOs who are celebrated for faster revenue and growth despite buggy systems in production because no one is dying.

Flights have crashed when pilots are fatigued, and they hit the runway too late and overshot it, similar to how many releases suffer when people on the project are fatigued and the Product Owner introduces a last-minute addition to the release.

Some flight crashes are attributed to sensors misleading the pilots, making a wrong decision, similar to how some leaders break what is working for them in testing, based on their listening to what works for other companies.

Computer models and simulations of plane crash scenario recreation do not usually consider human factors, such as how it happened during the investigation of a US Airways plane that landed on the Hudson River by Captain Sullenberger without crashing it. Initially, the computer model suggested the flight could have landed successfully at a nearby airport, but once human factors were added, it clearly showed the plane would have crashed. This works similarly to how some people react to bugs in production - once known, they say, "oh, this was so obvious, how on Earth can anyone miss this?" They are oblivious to the human factors of a tester, pressures, multiple things to do, other high-priority issues to be found, and coverage to be focused on.

Some commercial plane crashes are attributed to communication errors between the pilots and ATC, and that's what can happen with all other things being fine. Similarly, the requirement, product, and engineering can all be fine, and one communication error can make a release go bad.

The culture of the captain overriding the first officer's observation or warning has caused many plane crashes, forcing certain airlines with poor safety records to retrain their first officers to put the food down when the captain is compromising safety, and the captain to respect the first officer. Similarly, some decision-makers in the software industry behave like captains who override the observations testers are reporting, but unlike in the airline industry, there is no training that happens to decision-makers to respect testers.

Pilots need training to deal with situations of engine failure, sensor failure, autopilot failure, and tough weather conditions to be qualified to transport others, similar to how software needs to be exercised under conditions of failure to be qualified to be used by customers. Most developers testing their own code won't put their code through conditions of severe failure because of the attachment to their plane.

Test pilots who mimic a certain plane crash in a simulator need exceptional ability to recreate situations and actions. It is a highly intellectual and skilled job to be able to reproduce the crash scenario in a simulator, similar to how reproducing a bug that is happening for a customer requires skills and talent.

Test pilots are picked not just based on exceptional flying skills, but also based on their ability to communicate the problem effectively, similar to how top-notch testers don't just have exceptional testing skills, but also top-notch communication skills.

Poor maintenance is one of the contributing factors to air crashes, similar to how well-written but poorly maintained software will still fail at customers' hands.

The airline industry is a great example of how great AI works when it works, and how bad it fails when it fails, similar to how the software industry is slowly becoming.

Some flight crashes happen because the airplane or its components are well past their lifetime usage period. Similarly, software components that were strong once need to be relooked for maintenance, but most of the staffing and budgets are only built for new feature development, and the older components are forgotten.

An airline that makes good money escapes the effect of bad press on their business resulting from a plane crash and lives lost by pumping in a lot of marketing money post that episode, similar to how software companies with a lot of money cover up their data and privacy leaks with additional marketing spends.

Airline safety audit officers not being empowered to ground a plane is the most unsafe thing to happen to this world, similar to how some people call themselves "quality assurance" and don't assure any quality at all because to assure quality, one has to have the power to make a decision. In the airline industry, if the safety audit fails, a plane cannot fly, and in the software industry, many QAs have failed the software for a release, and it was still released, making the concept of QA a joke that no one laughs at, but everyone takes the joke as a serious thing.

All air crash investigations are not done within a deadline time frame to submit the final report. If done with a deadline, most of the conclusions would go wrong, and no useful feedback to plane manufacturers would come, resulting in more losses of lives. Similarly, in the software world, everything happens within a deadline, and hence the same problems recur within the software.

• • •

Politics & War

Politics and War

Like political parties with different and often conflicting ideologies, there are different schools of thought in testing, and the most popular one isn't always the most beneficial one, or the most vocal one isn't the one that represents the world.

Every political party says they are against corruption, just as every tech company says they want to build great quality software products. Saying makes them cool - not putting in the groundwork to translate it to reality makes them yet another.

The most talented people on Earth have lost elections to the least talented person because of popularity, money, and power they have, like how some of the most talented testers lose their ability to influence quality and testing in an organization to someone with a shallow idea of testing who holds power and title.

In large organizations, most quality initiatives die with time, like how political initiatives die because defending the titles and power become a priority.

One decision of a political leader in power can destroy several decades of heritage of a country, similar to how one leader of an org, with one decision, can wipe out all quality practices built over years. The leader never suffers - it is the people on the ground - both in politics and in any large organization.

Democracy has the same failure rate as other approaches to forming a government. Many enterprises, wanting to get a buy-in from multiple stakeholders to introduce a new tool, only bring tools that the majority vote for democratically, yet it has the same failure rate as the tools that weren't voted in.

The different schools of testing split people across the world and made them go against each other, similar to how political parties split people to fight against each other to enable their selfish motives of votes.

Political parties fight over each other, spreading false information to come to power, so that they can make more money, similar to how some office politics are power battles to decide who has the power to mess up testing in the org.

Wars between countries due to political conflict have not been able to kill a citizen's love for their own country, so modern-day politicians try killing the culture of a country to truly kill the country. Similarly, leaders in IT who kill the joy of testing eventually kill testing.

When two people with strong and often conflicting opinions about testing and automation work together, meetings end up looking like a presidential debate, influencing people to take sides.

A casual WhatsApp debate about different political beliefs has made friends into enemies, similar to how, in some testing conferences and over a casual LinkedIn post, two passionate people with different and diverse opinions have ended up offending each other.

Politicians talk about certain topics, knowing that citizens will be triggered to speak about them and hence bring their attention to the politician, similar to how some testers on LinkedIn constantly keep bringing up topics known for controversy for the sake of attention, without saying anything new about them.

Different political parties have different ideologies, and some political parties split and form two political parties with the same ideology, conflicting against each other, similar to how most automation enthusiasts conflict over whether to use XPath or not.

Politicians always talk as if they care for people, but truly, they care for people's tax money, similar to how some leaders in an organization seem to talk a lot about quality but care for money.

In most countries, the hardest-working class part with more valuable tax money than those who are having generational wealth, similar to how humans testing software are treated. Organizations get the laborious part of testing done by them and pay them the least in the name of "this is not an intellectual work" and "it can be automated anyway."

When a country decides to go to war or is forced into it, the ones living in the border area of the country are most affected, similar to how when a release goes bad, the people at the border of all functions (testers) are the most affected (most often in cultures that pin a Tester to be a QA).

Wars don't bring peace; it only brings one person's view of peace, not the citizens' view of peace. Similarly, conflicts between testers and other functions don't bring quality; it brings one person's notion of quality or speed in the aftermath, not the customer's view.

Wars don't help the global economy; they only help politicians go into the history books forever. Similarly, the heroic efforts of a QA team to improve quality don't improve quality; only cross-team work does.

There is peace amidst continuous wars in this world, in some places on this Earth; similarly, in the ocean of apps people use, the software we build should be the spot where they feel peace. Enough people are building war zones through their apps.

A war happening in one part of the world affects other parts of the world too, but the impact is not felt immediately.

Similarly, a bug in one component of the software may not affect another component immediately, but it surely will over time.

Photography

Photography

Photography is an art, and not everyone with a camera is a photographer, similar to how testing is an art, and not everyone who knows how to use a tool is a tester.

Wildlife photographers wait long hours for one good shot, similar to how some good testers run long-haul tests to catch one good bug, and most testers want to finish a sprint and give a sign-off.

Focus on a camera works like the expected result in test cases. They defocus on something and focus on something else. There can be a bug hiding in the defocused area, and that's the problem with heavily scripted test cases that makes humans miss such bugs while the focused area gets passed.

Digital cameras and AI make many people look like they are great photographers, but those who are made to look good know - inside, they are hollow, similar to how AI and Agentic testing can make companies look modern in their approach to testing, but deep inside, they know they don't understand why they still can't fix their quality issues.

Photographers who take time to adjust shutter speed, ISO, focus, aperture, and lens choice are truly enjoying what they are doing, similar to how some hands-on testers enjoy understanding, questioning, critical thinking, setting up an experiment, running, and observing a test. They don't want to automate what they are enjoying.

A drone operator is not necessarily a photographer, similar to how a tool operator in testing is not a tester.

A person uses filters on their photo to feel good about themselves, similar to how some companies use AI automation and tools to feel good that they too are doing great testing. The reality remains in the mirror.

Lighting plays a key role in capturing a good photo, similar to how budget plays a key role in performing good testing.

A good photographer and a good tester do similar things. They don't produce anything, but they capture what is already produced and present it in a way for the world to be moved, and that becomes their product.

Even the best photographer's work needs a commentary from someone like Richard Attenborough to make it more engaging, similar to how good testing requires a good commentary in an org to highlight the value of such good testing. Most organizations and leaders in testing lack the commentary skills and make their strong testing story look weak to others.

A good photographer knows what to not focus on, similar to how a good tester knows what not to focus on in a sprint, and bad testers (or leaders) try focusing on everything.

There are cameras with motion detection and capture that require no humans and can take pics of a tiger in the forest. If the purpose is to just capture a photo of a tiger, automated cameras work, but if the purpose is to also admire the tiger through the photo, a human needs to be in place. Most test execution can be automated, but to understand the experience of traversing those steps, a human needs to be in place.

All events that have drones also have traditional photographers, and people still cherish the traditional photographer's photos.

Candid pictures are the most wonderful ones, and like that, catching bugs candidly through freestyle exploratory testing is always fun. Making the bug pose through a test case and then capturing it is a boring way, but it works too. Just that alone will be boring.

A good professional-level photograph involves taking the picture, which is 50% of the job, and the remaining 50% lies in processing and editing it. This is similar to how good bug reporting is 50% recognizing the bug. Only when the other 50% work of investigating it and reporting it influentially is done, a bug truly stands out.

Some people are very bad at taking pictures – they don't center the subject well, their fingers come in between, they shake too much and capture unnecessary things into the frame, similar to how some testers are bad at reporting – they don't focus on the right thing, add too much unnecessary documentation, and mix it with things not required.

Camera equipment and lenses are built with a lot of controllability to let expert photographers tune them based on the need, unlike software that is built without testability, preventing even test experts from being able to test effectively.

High-end smartphones market themselves as the ones with the best camera, showcasing that a 60 fps 4K video and photos of wildlife can be captured. Most people buy that and use it mostly to take selfies in the bathroom, similar to how modern testing tools market high-value use cases. People end up using it for running an automated test that was running anyway, without the need for a modern new tool.

Drone cameras are complementary to the whole photography and videography because they provide an angle traditional cameras don't. Similarly, AI is complementary to testing. Since it is a new angle, everyone's obsessed about it.

Cooking & Baking

Cooking and Baking

The difference between a cook and a chef is, the cook just executes what is told and hence paid accordingly, and a chef architects the kitchen, menu, and recipe, and sets high standards for other budding chefs to follow. Similar to how testers who test because they need a job differ from testers who test because they care for customers and architect testing to bring value.

The person who wrote the recipe, preparing the same food, and the person who is merely following the recipe, preparing the same food, will have two different tastes, similar to someone having thought a test, running that test, to someone just running the test someone else thought.

Improvisation to an existing food recipe is a skill in itself, as much as improvising a test previously run to find something more insightful out of it.

Cooking is tough for many people and very therapeutic to others. Cleaning is tough for many people who feel cooking is therapeutic, similar to how coding is tough for many people and very therapeutic to others, and testing is tough for even those people.

The increase of business to Uber Eats, Doordash, Swiggy, and Zomato shows that people either don't have time to cook or don't like to cook. This fuels an industry of pharma companies growth because eating out is attributed to major health issues. Similarly, the world is overusing automation and AI to test, because there's no time to test to release faster, which ends up growing the team size of regression testing as product complexity grows.

Fine dining restaurants present the food in a certain way that appeals to our eyes. We get to see the food, and we pay a premium price for the plating, similar to how a premium is paid to those who present the information they have found through testing in a way that is easy for decision-makers to consume and make decisions.

Anything we cook, we can taste it at different stages of cooking and alter the taste as we cook, but that doesn't happen with baking. Once put into the OTG, it always leads to a binary result, similar to how testing software application and testing software that has a hardware dependency is. Once the hardware is shipped, altering it over the air is a task in itself.

Baking is a precise form of cooking. One ingredient in a slightly wrong proportion delivers a completely useless result, similar to how reproducing an intermittent bug is. It requires precision and controllability to alter a variable only to a specific degree to isolate some bugs. Even one degree off, the bug doesn't surface, and the application behaves normally.

Baking is like a science experiment - you either get an edible baked food or a non-edible baked food, unlike a test where even if it helps a human catch a bug or not, there's some value in it in the form of coverage.

A different wheat type produces different results in baking, despite the measurements and process being identical, similar to how different testers and different environments produce different results, even if the same test is performed in an identical fashion.

A good bread is the most difficult thing to bake because it has several stages of baking, requires time to be given to each stage, requires precision and plenty of practice. Cookies are relatively easier among all bakes, similar to tests that cannot be automated because of plenty of configuration and setup requirements being the hardest tests to run, while tests that can be automated are usually easy ones to run.

AI robots have come into existence today that cook ramen/noodles in five minutes when ingredients are stored and can be bought over a kiosk. However, even if AI is applied to a baking kiosk, it will take its own sweet time. Similarly, most checks to some degree can be automated, and most tests and user scenarios, even if automated, will take as much time or, in some cases, more time than humans running it.

A bread continues its important and final leg of baking during the cooling phase after it is taken from the oven, similar to how testing of a release is done only after sufficient testing continues on production servers once code changes are pushed to production. Basic checks don't cut it. From the outside, many breads look great, but inside the cooking might be incomplete.

Mass-produced foods that are processed and packaged aren't good for health, yet that's commercially made accessible everywhere, driving mass consumption. Similar to how AI tools are now mass-producing tests, the world is likely to consume more of it because of its ease and abundance.

There's a joy of eating biryani that most people have experienced, and there's a joy of cooking biryani that only a few have, similar to how most testers have the experience of using tools and not building one.

Canned and deep-frozen foods can be consumed over a long time after refrigeration, but they don't come close to freshly cooked food, similar to how a set of automated tests can continuously run for a long time, but the value of running fresh tests is always special.

Some foods are easy to cook, but very difficult to prepare, and some foods are tough to cook and easy to prepare, similar to how some tests are easy to run but tough to set up, and other tests are easy to set up and tough to run.

Passionate bakers enjoy creating new bakes and can get bored repeating the same thing over and over again, similar to how passionate testers like running new kinds of tests and being exposed to new contexts, rather than repeating the same thing over and over again.

Baking is a different specialized department of the overall kitchen inside a fine-dine restaurant, similar to how human-driven testing is a specialized department within the whole engineering unit. Treating it like - "this Tandoori chef can also bake cakes since he is free now" leads to bad Tandoori food and very poor-quality cakes.

Pastries are not baked, although many bakeries make and stock them, leading people who don't know baking to think that pastries are baked. Similarly, people who don't know testing think automation is testing and done in the same way as testing. If automation were testing, then people wouldn't be calling it "test-automation." That would be like saying "testing-testing" or "automation-automation."

Writing & Publishing

Writing and Publishing

Writing is hard. Even for people who can speak well, when it comes to writing, they get stuck, similar to how testing is. Very easy to speak about testing and pose like an expert, but doing it is very hard.

Writing comes from the practice of writing, and so does testing. When people keep away from the practice part, what they write or test can be replaced with ChatGPT or Claude.

Most celebrities who have published a book after becoming a celebrity didn't write the book. They hired someone, shared their stories, and a ghostwriter converted their stories into a book. Similarly, most large tech companies with a lot of money in the bank who brag that they make releases without needing testers have an agency that does their outsourced testing.

Writing involves gathering thoughts, structuring, writing, pausing, and then reflecting before writing more, similar to how some tests require us to pause and reflect before going ahead to create a wonderful test. When reflection is removed from writing and testing, the output is shallow.

Those who can write an email and a document, can't write a book or a poem, similar to how those who can test front-end and APIs can't test at whitebox and code level.

Many people feel anxious hitting the "Send" button in an email because once the "Send" is hit, people realize they missed something or forgot an attachment, similar to how some realizations and bugs come only after a release is done (which is human). The options, similar to "Undo send" and "Are you missing an attachment?" checks, can be automated but not the value part of writing the email. Let's say ChatGPT can handle the value of writing part too, but sadly, such emails are not read by humans; they just get another AI to summarize it.

Writing requires cognitive structure, and instead of helping people build that structure, people building AI are trying to remove it from the world. Similar to how writing clean code and writing a clean test case require cognitive structure and a deep understanding of the software, modern-day AI tools are trying to remove it.

Publishing is a very anxious moment to many because they think it creates a final impression about them, and they want to look good all the time. Only those who have acknowledged they aren't good enough while continuing to publish and continuing to improve their writing skills become good enough. Similarly, only those who acknowledge their software quality level isn't good enough and are working to improve it will improve it. If people are blind to it, they won't.

Publishing is one of the ways to improve writing because publishing brings feedback and reviews. Similarly, releasing incrementally and then talking to users or observing them is the way to understand and learn if the increment is really helping users succeed with their tasks or not.

Self-publishing books has made many people published authors, demonstrating that removing red tape can bring more ideas out of the hood, similar to how cutting the red tape in an organization can truly bring out the skills of people.

Writing a tweet, a blog post, a white paper, an article, an e-book, and a book requires versatility similar to how thinking, architecting, setting up, and running a test of different depths require.

Authors require a safe feedback loop when publishing their book, which will constructively critique, support, and highlight the good things of the book. That safe feedback loop in a software company is called testing, and the people doing that are called testers. If testers end up just highlighting problems in software and not the good things, they are unsafe for the project.

Formatting is a key part of improving the readability of a written document, similar to how usability is the key part of functionality to use a software.

Writing comes from a flow, and even the best authors can get writer's block, similar to how even really good developers can get coder's block, and a tester can get tester's block.

Writers know that some good writing requires spontaneity, and without that, the world would be less exciting today. Similar to how some good tests are born out of spontaneity while testing, which today the world has removed because everything should be pre-scripted or run by an agent.

Writing a book can be a solo job, but publishing requires a lot of different people to come together to put a book out. Similarly, coding can be a solo job, but release requires a lot of people to come together, and a test team plays the central point to bring all stakeholders together to a common shared understanding.

The longer we write a book, the tougher it is to remember the context and connections, requiring plenty of re-reading to get the context back. Similarly, the longer a software has been in development, the tougher it gets for people on the project to understand the purpose and customers' viewpoint, and requires leadership to keep re-orienting them. Most leaders don't do this.

To write, we need clarity, and to have clarity, we need to write. Similarly, to test code, we need testability, and to build testability, we need to code.

Some books are easier to write, tough to get published, and tougher to market, similar to how some software is easy to build, difficult to take to the market, and even more difficult to market.

Something that is easy to read can be a very hard one to write. Similarly, a feature that is easy to use can be a hard one to test.

Weight Loss, Nutrition & Fasting

Weight Loss, Nutrition and Fasting

People sign up to a gym to lose weight, and a month later, they find their weight has increased because they are eating more due to hard workouts. This is similar to how many companies think that because they hired more testers and automators, their quality will automatically increase, even though they are trying to release faster and end up worsening their quality.

Weight loss requires a balance between protein, carbs, fats, fiber, and minerals, similar to how improving quality requires functionality, performance, usability, security, reliability, testability, and supportability.

Most people, without long-term discipline, lose weight and gain it back, similar to how most companies improve their quality and worsen it again because they lack the discipline to uphold practices.

Every nutrition coach has a different approach, and every nutritionist is mostly right. Changing the nutritionist frequently does not let the body get into a rhythm, similar to how companies with constant attrition and hiring new leaders lead to the system not being able to go into one rhythm to produce quality software.

A good workout, a well-balanced meal paired with poor sleep, fails to produce the necessary fitness and weight loss, similar to diligent quality practices during the sprint and pushing a build with last-minute fixes without sufficient testing time.

People want to lose fat and not weight, but they think they have lost fat by losing muscles, similar to how some companies think they have reduced costs and increased dev testing by letting go of all testers.

Having one large cheat meal usually takes away weeks of calorie deficit build-up, similar to how one sprint of "let's bypass sufficient testing" can wipe off many previous good sprint releases.

A weight scale showing a lower number is a north star for many people wanting to lose weight, but a north star can be achieved by compromising health, similar to how revenue is the north star for many companies, and they compromise quality and testing to get there.

The healthiest food is home-cooked food, but most people consume processed fast foods, leading to poor health. This is similar to how many organizations opt for fast testing solely through automation and end up with poor-quality issues. At one point in life, fast food becomes so addictive that people resort to taking tablets to treat diseases instead of making lifestyle changes.

Eating a fruit and drinking the same fruit juice have two different nutritional values, similar to how the result varies when a human runs a test and the same test is automated and run by the automated script. They are not the same.

Most mothers are the biggest threat to a weight loss journey of their grown-up adult child, similar to how most founders are the biggest threat to building quality in a startup because they have the power to push anything they want at any time in their timeline of urgency.

Helping people lose weight is a huge market, giving rise to many companies that produce promising-looking initial results through a lack of deep understanding of the human body, hormonal imbalances, and metabolism. This is accompanied by adverse side effects and long-term health issues, similar to how quality is a big business and many companies exist to provide notional quality.

Some people lose weight to improve their health, and some people lose weight to look good in front of a few people, similar to how some companies focus on quality because they care for customers, and others focus on quality to please a customer who has expressed dissatisfaction.

A fat loss journey constantly hits a saturation point every few pounds of loss, and tests if one is consistent before the next drop, similar to how improving quality at an org will hit saturation and test if people are consistent before bringing the next big jump in quality.

Some people misunderstand a supplement to be a food in itself and consume large quantities of it, similar to how organizations treat AI or automation. They are supplements to the human-driven approach to testing, not a replacement, and when they consume large quantities of it, they will live with the side effects of it.

Google trends indicate that a decade ago, no one bothered about intermittent fasting. But when a scientist received a Nobel Prize for it, people started searching and following it. Similar to how, in the testing world, a decade ago, the world didn't bother sufficiently about context-driven testing. Now, once AI emerged, suddenly people who didn't want to speak about it now say context is everything for testing using AI.

Strength Training & Body Building

Strength Training and Body Building

Coding is like working on biceps, chest, and shoulders, whereas testing is like a leg workout. Even people who love working out dread the leg workouts. Without a good mix of leg workout, core, and upper body, most people and software would look like Johnny Bravo.

Among the bodybuilding community, there is a confusion and bias against cardio exercises, where most people lean toward the idea that cardio is against muscle growth, and a minority who think a hybrid workout is beneficial to overall growth. Similar to how in the world of testing, the majority lean toward AI and Automation as a way forward in testing, with a minority that believes in a hybrid approach.

Steroids and workouts pump the muscles up to the point that people taking steroids start self-admiration of their mega increase of their muscles, which leads to addiction, similar to how some IT industry leaders get a high by releasing complex features in a short span, making their team work until burnout, and then rewarding them for burnout so that people want to burn themselves out again and again.

Resistance training is very important for muscle growth, and that's how muscles become stronger, similar to how software and companies become stronger by respecting testers who resist certain things being done to software in the name of business.

Adding too much resistance and too much weight causes tears in the muscles or ligaments, similar to how some testers apply more resistance than necessary, thus defeating the purpose for which they were hired.

Some people add weights to pump their muscles, and some people add weight to pump their ego, similar to how some people add tests to improve coverage, and some people add tests to please a leader who wants to see more tests added.

Squats and deadlifts are the kind of workouts that engage the core, upper body, and legs, similar to how reliability and long-haul tests are good to test functionality and performance at the same time.

People trying to get rid of testing in companies are like people trying to get rid of the mirror in the gym because it is slowing down people from working out, as the mirror makes people spend time posing between sets. If the mirrors are removed from gyms, many gyms would lose their businesses.

A mirror in the gym helps in two ways - to self-assess the form of the workout and then to self-motivate, looking at the muscle pump, similar to how testing helps self-assess the value of what is being built and also to build confidence in making a release decision.

A great body can be built with fewer weights and more reps, and also with heavy weights and fewer reps, similar to how testing can be done with fewer tests driven by good test design, or more tests with poor test design. One of them feeds the ego, so the world is drawn toward it.

Strength training is so addictive that people can overdo it and injure themselves permanently, so it is required to tread with caution. Similar to how automation is so addictive, people can end up overdoing it and making customers the only source of truth, damaging their reputation forever.

One can spend a lot of time in the gym, looking at a phone, talking to people, listening to music, moving around, and end up doing very little volume of workout, similar to how some people spend a lot of time at work, talking to people in meetings, chatting about work over chai, answering Slack messages, and doing very little volume of work per day.

Even people who work out continuously find it hard to break the fat from the tummy, and that's often the last place where the fat is burned. Similarly, tech debt of testability, once accumulated, remains in the belly of the software.

Rest, recovery, and hydration play a vital role in muscle building. People who don't rest well often develop muscle soreness and, at times, muscle injuries that require months of rehab, similar to how engineers in startups, who slog release after release, break their own capabilities and their future after a certain time.

A spotter's job in a gym is to be there as a support system to someone pushing their limits, catching the weight before the point of failure. That's similar to how a tester focused on observability in production should work and behave.

Working out the same muscle every day fatigues it, makes it sore, and injures it. Hence, people who work out have a schedule of different muscles on different days. Similarly, testing the functionality of software over and over again fatigues people working on the project. There are other quality criteria that matter for the business too, but the software industry largely works on fatigue.

Most people obsessed with muscle building and working out in the gym five days a week focus a lot on their diet because they know diet is where 33% of the muscle building happens. Similarly, those who are obsessed with quality focus not just on code quality, but on the quality of the understood, documented, and communicated requirements because that contributes to 33% of quality.

From the outside, the life of someone obsessed with working out regularly looks like a sick life. They stick to sleep schedules, skip eating carb-heavy foods at parties, and maybe skip parties too. Similarly, people obsessed about quality live such a life too; they take extra care to format their code to make it readable, want a certain button length precisely the way the designer gave it, and the experience for a customer to be consistently flawless. Without some people living such a sick life, this world would be a disaster.

Building quality in a software product and building a heavy, muscular body are similar. It requires obsession. Casual, “I too work out regularly,” doesn’t cut it.

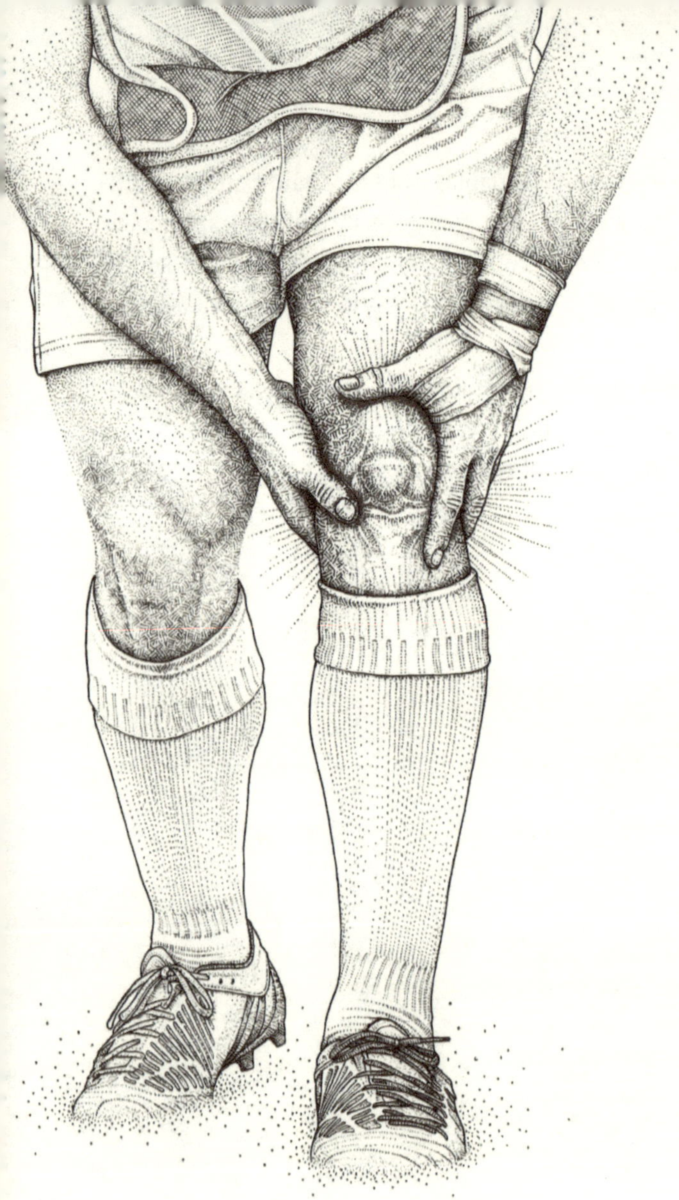

Sport Injuries & Rehab

Sport Injuries and Rehab

A fracture is like a bug in code that can be fixed sooner than a ligament tear, which is like a bug in the architecture or culture of the company that requires careful rehab and discipline to fix it.

A muscle spasm can happen to people who warm up, stretch, hydrate, and rest well, similar to how dips in quality can happen to organizations that are doing everything right. Those who have a well-structured approach to rehab come out stronger; otherwise, it ends up being the beginning of a downfall.

Being away from sports after an injury is the hardest part of life, similar to how being away from hands-on testing or coding after promotion to a manager role. For some people, promotion is an injury until they get rehab done.

Many people fear getting surgery done and try to cope with the injury until it becomes painful enough and worse, like how many companies fear re-architecture will slow them down from releasing features and keep accumulating tech debt until one day it becomes too expensive.

Poor bug fixes act like a painkiller. People make a software release, thinking the bug has been fixed, only to find the bug they thought had gone came back again in the next release.

The more active a person is, the more likely injuries are, and they have to be dealt with immediately to prevent a build-up and completely being asked to stop. Similarly, more actively built software will have bugs creeping in, and if most of them are pushed into backlogs, they would end up preventing new features from being built in a clean way.

Rehabilitation is boring, painful, and there are no shortcuts or faster ways to recover from an injury, just like building quality.

Fixing a broken ligament and bone requires the help of a surgeon and a physiotherapist. Win or lose, it is a team effort, similar to how a developer and tester are for the quality of code.

Fixing a broken ligament is a team work, beginning with the radiologist, doctor, surgeon, nurse, and physiotherapist, but the main credit goes to the surgeon, who are doctors, just like how building quality is a team work in software, but the credit goes to one subgroup of people if things work well, and others look incidental.

The way humans handle rehab is by making some progress, feeling excited about the progress, and then overdoing something and having to take two steps back. They then work toward the previous good state, just like how people overdo some good thing in building software that works for them until it breaks. They then have to go back a few steps. Provided the overdoing is within a limit of two steps back, but most often software engineers overdo things that require ten steps back, and they don't want to go back, causing regression issues with every step forward.

Injury and rehab force people who weren't disciplined in their life to become disciplined in their life to remove pain because there is no other option in front of them, unlike in the software world. People who experience pain of dealing with consistent poor code quality and a culture of indiscipline switch their employer for temporary relief.

The fitness level before an injury plays a vital role in determining how well someone recovers from an injury and rehab, similar to the state of quality of software prior to a bug fix, determines the improvement of quality of software after a bug fix.

There's a difference between a person whose profession is sports getting injured and a person who is working on computers getting injured while playing sports, similar to how there is a difference between a startup software having critical bugs and a large enterprise software having critical bugs. Large enterprises have money to take that shock, some startups fold permanently due to bugs.

Injuries are sometimes a way for us to discover and learn about how different muscles and ligaments work in ways to support us, similar to how investigating a bug is sometimes a wonderful opportunity to learn how different subsystems interact with each other in the software we are testing, as opposed to what people thought it did.

Some bug fixes are like ligament reconstruction surgeries, and testing those bug fixes is like post-surgery rehab. Surgery lasts two hours, and physiotherapy lasts several months.

Occasionally, when a physiotherapist sees their patient making good progress, they are likely to push more for faster results that might delay the progress, similar to how some leaders in IT push for faster results when they see an approach working and get surprised when it fails to deliver value. Pushing is an inherent nature of humans. Fifty percent of the time it produces good results, and the rest 50% are failures.

When there is one muscle that gets injured, all adjacent muscles fatigue and can get injured too because the load on them is higher, trying to compensate for the injured muscle. Similarly, if one component in software is buggy but others are good, bugs still manifest every time those components interact with the buggy one.

Many top sports players have had major sports injuries and have recovered well, come back, and competed, and even won world championships, similar to how some companies that have a culture of quality will always bounce back from any technical glitch.

When a particular leg suffers an injury and needs a long rehab time, the other leg usually has taken a hit by the time the injured leg is in shape. Similarly, in software, if one portion of the software is buggy, by the time they get addressed, it often comes at the cost of a portion that wasn't buggy before needing attention because it was underserved by humans building and testing it.

The average recovery time of a teen, an adult, a middle-aged person, and a senior citizen is all different for the same injury, similar to how long it would take to test the fix of a bug in software that is recently built to legacy code.

A physiotherapist's job is to get their patient to a level where the need for a physio disappears, but the exercises continue, similar to how a test consultant's job should be about getting their client to the point where they don't need the consultant anymore, but the practices influenced by the consultant continue.

Yoga & Meditation

Yoga and Meditation

Yoga is a union of different entities that make us similar to how holistic test coverage is an assessment of different entities of the usefulness of a software to its customers.

Holding a pose in hatha yoga requires stability, and some people can hold it for a few seconds, while others can hold it for a few minutes, similar to how software needs to maintain its usefulness state for a long time for its users. Most software looks good on the surface and for happy paths because it can hold up for initial usage, but only a very few software can truly sustain it when used deeply, also because most testing is done at a surface level.

Yoga is a way of living, and not just the poses, similar to how building software quality is a culture of a company, and not just in how much testing or automation is being done.

Different poses of yoga are like different types of tests. Most people do just a few poses and consider themselves to be yoga practitioners, similar to how most companies do functional or requirement validation testing and consider their software tested good enough.

Yoga calms the body and mind, preparing them to be suitable for meditation, similar to how testing is a preparation toward quality, but isn't quality itself.

Modern-day commercial yoga studios popularized and marketed power yoga to influence people to see power yoga as a combination of weight loss exercises, strength training, and yet yoga, similar to how the software industry tried to create a full-stack engineer as a combination of front-end, back end, coding, testing, and support. Over time, the market for power yoga has faded.

Most meditation techniques focus on breathing and observing our own breath, similar to how people testing software should regularly sit and observe their customers using (and struggling with) their software through analytics. They would end up discovering that their test coverage and customer usage are in two different places with limited overlap.

Practice of yoga enables the body to sit in one posture for a long duration, enabling deep meditation, similar to how the practices of quality in an org enable people to build growth without drama.

People immediately feel good after doing yoga and meditation because it slows them down, and that's the feeling they are denying themselves at work by going faster and faster.

Meditation brings detachment, and detachment clears the mind from the clutter, similar to how refactoring and optimizing the code bring clarity to the structure of the code, making it more testable and debuggable.

Consistent yoga practices can prevent certain diseases and injuries, similar to how holistic test coverage can prevent certain bugs and problems from happening to the software.

Yoga is repackaged and sold in different commercial forms in the modern world, like how preventing bugs is sold as shift left. It existed in its raw form before it was packaged and sold that way, but the modern world demands and requires repackaging to make old things look very exciting.

The cat and cow pose are the two basic forms of poses in yoga, originally called Marjaryasana and Bitilasana, which people found hard to remember. Hence, cat and cow became popular. Similarly, foundational test design techniques are getting lost because it isn't cool to say it. But when AI uses it, hopefully, someone will re-package it and make it cool again.

Meditation helps us to be away from ourselves and see things objectively, without bringing emotions into it. It is testing, a way to remove the bias and inattentional blindness of people building software and seeing things objectively.

There are a few hundred channels today on YouTube, all teaching yoga, but very few teaching meditation. Similar to how there are plenty of channels on YouTube teaching people how to automate or use tools, and very few channels on how to test software or care for customers as a tester.

Taking pics and videos of our yoga practice and posting it is Instagram brag-worthy content, while doing meditation and posting it is not. Similarly, automation and AI are LinkedIn brag-worthy content, and testing is not.

Buddhist monks in monasteries live a life that appears as if every day is a repetition of the previous day, and they are doing that to find salvation. Similarly, while we all love to automate repetitive tasks, we forget that we are doing it to find the work that is repetitive but lovely to do for our career salvation.

To be in a meditative state isn't just when we sit with eyes closed, but also one can be in a meditative state even when eyes are open and walking. Similarly, doing testing doesn't mean in front of the software only; it can also be done while in a meeting, hearing someone make an assumption about what the customer would not do.

Vipassana is a meditation technique to observe, self-reflect, and transform ourselves. Similarly, testing (done correctly) is a way to observe, self-reflect, and transform the product we are building.

Everything Else

Everything Else

Quality problems are similar to dental problems. Most of them are only found just when the root canal is the only way forward. A good daily dental hygiene prevents many such root canals, but people never stop at one root canal, do they?

When people who lived in a country where they could afford a house help move to another country where they have to clean their own toilet, they find it super difficult, just like how developers feel when they are asked to test after the testers are let go.

Test Automation obsession in the IT industry is like an obsession with biryani. People obsessing over eating biryani are not bothered about health - they are doing it for the fun of it.

There are hundreds of types of biryani, and a true biryani lover will not dislike a type of biryani but may have a favorite. Unlike in the testing world, there are several different approaches to testing, but people who love testing are highly opinionated about which type of testing is good and that others are not so good.

Most people can set up their own nano-brewery of beer and coffee at home, but they prefer instant ones after they discover how hard it is to brew unless they are really passionate about it, similar to how most testers get excited about open-source tools. Then, when they are tested on their passion and skills to modify it to suit their needs, they navigate toward free instant software.

Whiskey drinkers graduate from cheap whiskey that gets them a high to a blended scotch and single malt. It takes a special kind of skill in drinking whiskey to appreciate a single malt. Similarly, most testers start with thinking executing shallow tests, and it takes a special artistic skill to come up with deep value tests and perform them (instead of executing them).

Different tests for the same feature are like different levels of the astrology charts of the same person, revealing hidden things. A planet may be exalted in D1 chart and debilitated in D9 chart; similarly, a feature may appear to work well in the front-end but can be causing a performance bottleneck in the back end with continuous usage.

Many football matches come down to penalty shootouts, where the goalkeeper determines the larger part of win or lose for the team. Yet, the most celebrated and popular players in the world are forwards like Lionel Messi and Cristiano Ronaldo, similar to how testers play a crucial part in some complex release situations to make a team win, yet will be a part of a cost-cut move.

There are people who live healthily because of technology, since they know what healthy means, and there are people who get sick by using technology because they don't know what healthy means. Similarly, there will be companies who produce good quality software in the post-AI world because they understand quality, and most will produce poor-quality software using AI because they don't understand quality.

Smoking and drinking are injurious to health, but are done as recreational activities, and people think of them as social things to make friends. Similarly, practices like "shift left" have ended up as a cool thing to do to stay relevant rather than to really improve the quality.

Beautiful gardens are built over years of nurturing, seeing growth happen slowly and pruning; similarly, great quality software is only built over the years of nurturing and pruning. People skip the pruning and expect quality to happen. Never.

Don’t let AI, or anything else, take the joy of testing away from you.

If it does, you never had the joy in the first place.

Aristotle, 350 BC

www.ingramcontent.com/pod-product-compliance
Lightning Source LLC
LaVergne TN
LVHW100320210926
848480LV00003B/1192
* 9 7 9 8 9 0 3 6 2 6 4 8 9 *